DEPARTMENT OF STATE INTERNATIONAL CYBERSPACE POLICY STRATEGY

March 2016

Public Law 114-113, Division N, Title IV, Section 402

Introduction

On December 18, 2015, the President signed into law the Consolidated Appropriations Act, 2016, as Public Law 114-113, which contained a reporting requirement (Division N, Section 402) with respect to the Department's international cyberspace policy efforts, particularly those related to norms of state behavior. Section 402(b) seeks information on actions and activities undertaken to implement the President's 2011 U.S. *International Strategy for Cyberspace (International Strategy)*, efforts to promote norms of state behavior in cyberspace, alternative concepts for norms promoted by certain other countries, threats facing the United States, tools available to the President to deter malicious actors, and resources required to build international norms. This *Department of State International Cyberspace Policy Strategy* (Strategy), therefore, notes significant items of progress in implementing the President's *International Strategy* and reflects three themes: the applicability of international law; the importance of promoting confidence building measures; and the significant progress the Department has made, working in partnership with other federal departments and agencies, to promote international norms of state behavior in cyberspace, as well as future plans in this area. The Strategy, prepared by the Department of State, is being submitted to the Committee on Foreign Relations of the United States Senate and the Committee on Foreign Affairs of the House of Representatives.

Sec. 402(b)(1) – A review of actions and activities undertaken by the Secretary of State to date to support the goal of the President's International Strategy for Cyberspace, released in May 2011, to "work internationally to promote an open, interoperable, secure, and reliable information and communications infrastructure that supports international trade and commerce, strengthens international security, and fosters free expression and innovation."

The U.S. Department of State leads the U.S. government's diplomatic and development engagement on a wide range of activities in cyberspace, and is a leading participant in the whole-of-government approach to achieve foreign policy and national security objectives in this rapidly evolving and expanding area. As cyber issues have dramatically grown in global importance over the last five years, the Department of State has prioritized efforts to mainstream cyberspace policy issues in all our diplomatic activities and embrace it as a new foreign policy imperative. The Department's cyberspace policy efforts are firmly grounded in the President's *International Strategy*, which states the U.S. goal "to promote an open, interoperable, secure, and reliable information and communications infrastructure that supports international trade and commerce, strengthens international security, and fosters free expression and innovation."

The Department of State structures its cyberspace diplomacy around interrelated, dynamic, and cross-cutting policy priorities drawn from the President's *International Strategy*. Since the *International Strategy's* release, the Department and our interagency partners have made significant strides in implementing its goals across all of these priority pillars, discussed separately below. For each policy priority, we have highlighted select accomplishments from our robust bilateral and multilateral diplomatic engagement since early 2011.

Digital Economy

The Department of State, in partnership with other federal departments and agencies, works bilaterally and multilaterally, as well as at regional and global levels, to lead and shape the international debate around achieving an open, secure, interoperable, and reliable Internet; confronting market access barriers that restrict the importation of U.S. information and communication technology (ICT) goods and services, and working to prevent the creation of new barriers, such as data localization and "duty of care" requirements; and promoting trans-border data flows. The Department of State, in coordination with the Department of Commerce and the interagency, also plays a leading role in fostering collaboration between the public and private sector to develop international standards and share best practices that enable innovation; facilitating interoperability, security, and resiliency; improving trust in online transactions; and spurring competition in global markets.

Accomplishments:

- Negotiated the Organisation for Economic Co-operation and Development Principles for Internet Policymaking (2011), as well as updates to the "privacy guidelines" (2013) and "security guidelines" (2014), which advance strategies aimed at promoting sound Internet policy practices and managing privacy and digital security risk toward economic and social prosperity. The Department of Commerce served as the secretariat for the interagency effort for the Principles for Internet Policymaking, and interagency partners engaged in all these negotiations.

- Achieved ministerial commitments, advanced policies to increase broadband access and facilitate the free flow of information across borders, and developed global ICT standards through engagements in international organizations, including the Asia-Pacific Economic Cooperation (APEC) and the International Telecommunication Union (ITU), which included participation by more than 60 Department-led, accredited public-private delegations.
- Negotiated updates to the Radio Regulations – the international treaty that governs the use of the radio frequency spectrum and satellite orbits – to enable the evolution of mobile broadband, unmanned aircraft systems, and space-based systems promoting U.S. economic growth and innovation.
- Prevented efforts to enact data localization requirements in several instances through focused diplomatic engagement.
- Worked with the Department of Commerce and other interagency partners to facilitate the successful negotiation of the EU-U.S. Privacy Shield Framework with the European Commission (to replace the U.S.-EU Safe Harbor Framework).

International Security

Many states are developing military cyberspace capabilities, a prospect that is increasingly viewed as threatening to both our national and international security. Key aspects of cyberspace – such as the difficulty of attributing an attack to its perpetrators or sponsors, and the dual-use nature of the technology – are seen by many as inherently destabilizing. While emphasizing that existing international law applies to state behavior in cyberspace, the Department of State has pioneered the promotion of a framework of shared voluntary norms to guide state behavior in peacetime, and advanced the development of practical cyber confidence building measures (CBMs) to reduce risk, with the objective of establishing a coalition of states in support of that framework.
Accomplishments:

- Achieved 2015 Group of 20 (G20) Leaders' commitments to affirm the applicability of international law to state behavior in cyberspace, refrain from cyber-enabled theft of intellectual property for commercial gain, and endorse the view that all states should abide by norms of responsible behavior.

- Adoption of U.S.-championed framework of international cyber stability through pivotal negotiations in the United Nations Group of Governmental Experts on Developments in the Field of Information and Telecommunications in the Context of International Security in 2013 and 2015 that resulted, *inter alia*, in the affirmation of the applicability of existing international law, including the United Nations Charter, to state conduct in cyberspace and the articulation of voluntary peacetime norms of state behavior.
- Reached agreement in 2013 and 2016 and have begun implementation in the Organization for Security and Cooperation in Europe (OSCE) of CBMs to build trust and reduce the risk of escalation and misperception in the region. Also reached agreement in the ASEAN Regional Forum in 2015 on a detailed work plan with a proposed set of CBMs for future implementation.
- Reached consensus at the 2014 North Atlantic Treaty Organization (NATO) Wales Summit on a statement affirming that international law applies to state behavior in cyberspace, and cyber defense is part of NATO's collective defense mission.

Promoting Cybersecurity Due Diligence

Cybersecurity is critical to global security, and all nations have a responsibility to promote it by protecting their own networks and information infrastructure to ensure they are secure, reliable, and resilient. U.S. cybersecurity priorities include promoting widespread adoption of cybersecurity best practices and frameworks, including national strategies, computer security incident response teams (CSIRTs), public-private partnerships, and public awareness campaigns. The Department of State is expanding bilateral cybersecurity cooperation with like-minded countries and supporting multilateral efforts to improve cooperation on network defense, information sharing, and incident management and recovery. We also are leveraging foreign assistance tools and resources to develop sustainable CSIRT capabilities by engaging stakeholders, assessing needs, and offering technical assistance to improve our collective ability to combat cyber threats. This assistance, pursued in partnership with the Department of Homeland Security and others, is critical to achieving the Administration's cybersecurity goals at the bilateral, regional, and global levels. These goals include creating a global culture of cybersecurity due diligence, reducing intrusions and disruptions affecting U.S. networks, ensuring the resiliency of information infrastructure, and improving the security of the high-tech supply chain.

In addition to promoting efforts to prevent and deter malicious cyber activity, it is essential to maintain and strengthen our country's resilience to a cyber incident. As noted in the February 9 White House announcement of the Cybersecurity National Action Plan, by this spring the Administration intends to "release a policy for national cyber incident coordination and an accompanying severity methodology for evaluating cyber incidents so that government agencies and the private sector can communicate effectively and provide an appropriate and consistent level of response."

Accomplishments:

- Worked with the National Institute of Standards and Technology to draft the Framework for Improving Critical Infrastructure Cybersecurity, which was developed in collaboration with the private sector and technical experts and incorporated international input, towards improving critical infrastructure cybersecurity through the use of voluntary security standards, guidelines, and practices.
- Launched global CSIRT capacity building efforts, including partnering with the Department of Homeland Security and the Forum of Incident Response and Security Teams to draft a CSIRT development framework, and initiated a CSIRT capacity building program via Carnegie Mellon University's Software Engineering Institute, with an initial focus on sub-Saharan Africa.
- Promoted the development of comprehensive national cyber policies and strategies globally, in close partnership with regional multilateral bodies, such as the Organization of American States (OAS) and the African Union Commission, and through a new capacity building initiative being developed for the Department of State by MITRE Corporation.
- Promoted the "Stop. Think. Connect." awareness campaign and National Cybersecurity Awareness Month internationally to build awareness and understanding in civil society through public outreach by embassies and consulates, in partnership with the Department of Homeland Security.

Combating Cybercrime

The Department of State, in partnership with the Department of Justice and the Department of Homeland Security, is a global leader in the campaign against transnational cybercrime. We actively partner with key allies and multilateral partners to help countries effectively utilize existing legal tools; fund and support U.S. law enforcement programs to develop modern legal frameworks; build specialized investigative, prosecutorial, judicial, and border and customs capabilities; provide training on cybercrime investigations to law enforcement officers in partner countries; and improve international cooperation mechanisms to more effectively combat modern, high-tech crime threats. We actively promote membership in the Council of Europe Convention on Cybercrime (Budapest Convention), to which the United States and 47 other countries are parties, and are the strongest supporter for the Group of Seven (G7) 24/7 Network, which provides investigators in 70 countries with dedicated points of contact who can provide urgent assistance with significant investigations involving electronic evidence.

Accomplishments:

- Helped to expand Budapest Convention membership by 17 countries since 2011, and to recruit another 10 countries that are actively working to become parties to the Convention. Promoted the Convention as a framework for numerous other countries.
- Enlarged the G7 24/7 Network, in partnership with the Department of Justice, to 70 countries as of February.
- Offered up to a total of $7.75 million in rewards for information through the Department's Transnational Organized Crime Program, leading to the arrest or conviction of five suspected leaders and members of transnational cybercrime organizations.

Internet Governance

The Department of State, in partnership with the Department of Commerce and others, actively participates in global efforts to ensure the multistakeholder model of Internet governance prevails against attempts to create state-centric frameworks, which would undermine openness and freedom, hinder innovation, and jeopardize the functionality of the Internet. The multistakeholder model is characterized by transparent, bottom-up, consensus-driven processes whereby all governments, the private sector, civil society, academia, and the technical community participate on equal footing, and which has been the primary source for the Internet's phenomenal growth. We continue to cultivate new partners in advancing this approach in various international fora.

Accomplishments:

- Advanced and preserved the multistakeholder approach to Internet governance, enabling the deployment of new technologies and services and the promotion of Internet openness and security in cyberspace at key international negotiations. These negotiations include the UN General Assembly's High Level Meeting on the Overall Review of the World Summit on the Information Society, which continues efforts to build an inclusive, people-centered, development-oriented Information Society (December 2015), as well as global engagements, such as the ITU Plenipotentiary Conference in Busan, South Korea (2014), NETmundial Global Multistakeholder Meeting on the Future of Internet Governance in São Paulo, Brazil (2014), the ITU World Telecommunication Policy Forum in Geneva, Switzerland (2013), and the World Conference on International Telecommunications in Dubai, United Arab Emirates (2012), among others.

- Worked with interagency counterparts in support of the Department of Commerce's announcement of its intent to transition the stewardship of key Internet functions to the multistakeholder community (March 2014), and engaged in a global, multistakeholder effort toward the stewardship transition and enhanced accountability of the Internet Corporation of Assigned Names and Numbers.
- Supported the Internet Governance Forum, the premier venue for global, multistakeholder dialogue on Internet policy issues, through substantive and financial contributions, and successfully negotiated its continued mandate.

Internet Freedom

The Department of State works tirelessly to ensure that the global Internet is an open platform on which to innovate, learn, organize, and express individual beliefs, free from undue interference or censorship. We have worked with key international partners to support successive UN Human Rights Council resolutions affirming that individuals have the same rights online as they do offline. We are a primary supporter and founding member of the Freedom Online Coalition, which has grown to 29 like-minded countries that work to advance Internet freedom through diplomatic coordination, and work closely with private sector and civil society partners to promote rights-respecting policies. We also are the leading global funder of Internet freedom programs to support anti-censorship and secure communications technology, promote digital safety in repressive environments, empower advocates who advance Internet freedom in their home countries and abroad, and support widely cited research that monitors and analyzes the technical and policy threats to Internet freedom. The Department of State works closely with the Department of Commerce and other agencies to promote the free flow of information and facilitate communications for people under repressive regimes, and engages closely with the private sector and civil society groups to ensure successful implementation of these efforts.

Accomplishments:

- Launched the Freedom Online Coalition as one of 15 founding countries in December 2011, and helped it expand to 29 countries as of February.
- Worked with partners to secure passage of the 2012 UN Human Rights Council resolution affirming that people have the same rights online as offline, and a 2014 resolution reaffirming the same principle.
- Invested, with USAID, more than $145 million since 2008 in technologies, training, research, and advocacy efforts to promote Internet freedom worldwide.
- Worked closely with the interagency to issue General Licenses for Personal Communications for the citizens of Iran (2013) and Sudan (2015).

International Development and Capacity Building

The Internet has proven to be a successful catalyst for economic and social development around much of the world, in large part due to its open, interoperable, secure, and reliable structure and its multistakeholder governance. The Department of State, in partnership with the interagency, utilizes an active, ongoing, and longstanding series of capacity building programs and consultations to expand Internet access and build the capacity of foreign governments across a range of interconnected cyberspace policy issues to combat cybercrime, counter violent extremism online, improve cooperation with global partners to address shared threats, promote a culture of cybersecurity, develop cyber confidence building measures, expand freedom online, and help developing countries improve domestic market and regulatory conditions to catalyze private sector investment. The Department of State is working to expand Internet access through innovation and initiatives like Global Connect and the Alliance for an Affordable Internet. The Department is also actively involved in promoting donor cooperation, including bilateral and multilateral participation in joint cyber capacity building initiatives.

Accomplishments:

- Launched the Global Connect initiative that seeks to bring online by 2020 1.5 billion people who are currently without Internet access.
- Funded since 2011, in close coordination with interagency partners, regional cybersecurity training workshops across sub-Saharan Africa to support less developed countries strengthen their laws, policies, and institutions in accordance with the multistakeholder approach. Additional efforts have been made across other key regions, including Southeast Asia and Latin America, in

donor partnerships with Japan and Australia, among others, and through contributions to efforts by multilateral organizations, such as the OAS, the Council of Europe, and the United Nations Office on Drugs and Crime.

- Provided, in partnership with the interagency, cybercrime and cybersecurity training to officials from 35 sub-Saharan African nations through a series of six Regional Economic Community-focused workshops, and also conducted cybercrime training for ASEAN countries, as well as countries within the Pacific Islands.
- Joined the Netherlands in founding the Global Forum on Cyber Expertise in 2015, a global platform for countries, international organizations, and the private sector to exchange best practices and expertise on cyber capacity building; and partnered with Japan, Australia, Canada, the African Union Commission, and Symantec on four cybersecurity and cybercrime capacity building initiatives.
- Funded and promoted the creation and usage of a cybersecurity mobile laboratory through the OAS Inter-American Committee Against Terrorism, as well as other regional initiatives, to identify vulnerabilities, improve cybersecurity, and promote collaboration between the OAS and other organizations, such as the APEC and OSCE.
- Helped launch the Alliance for Affordable Internet in 2013, a public-private partnership working to catalyze policy change to drive down the cost of broadband and unlock rapid gains in Internet penetration rates around the world.
- Worked with interagency counterparts and the United States Telecommunications Training Institute to launch the *ICT Policymaking in a Global Environment and Cybersecurity Awareness Raising and Capacity Building* seminar providing training to 162 officials from developing and least developed countries as of December 31, 2015.
- Implemented significant regulatory changes, together with the interagency, to enhance access by the citizens of Cuba to ICTs, following the President's 2014 announcement on Cuba policy changes.
- Negotiated the "Dubai Action Plan" through the ITU, which set a robust four-year work plan to increase developing countries' capacity to use ICTs for economic growth.

Global, Cross-Cutting Cyber Issues

The advent of cyberspace policy as a foreign policy imperative has led to the creation of a broad range of new, cross-cutting bilateral and multilateral diplomatic engagements, as well as the integration of cyberspace issues into numerous existing diplomatic processes and fora, including at the presidential/leaders level. Many other foreign countries have followed our lead by drafting national cyber strategies, establishing cyber policy offices in their foreign ministries, establishing a cyber coordinator position within their foreign ministries, and elevating cyber policy to a top diplomatic priority. At the same time, cyber issues have gained significant traction in virtually every regional and global venue, including the Organization for Security and Cooperation in Europe, the Organization of American States, the ASEAN Regional Forum, and the United Nations. The Department of State, in partnership with the interagency, has spearheaded the creation of these new and emerging cyber policy circles, and actively works to advance U.S. strategic interests, in coordination with like-minded partners.

One of the Department of State's high-priority, cross-cutting cyber issues is its effort to counter violent extremism (CVE) online. As highlighted in the President's *International Strategy*, the United States counters terrorist narratives online by highlighting alternative viewpoints instead of suppressing speech, consistent with our core values, and we remain focused on criminal activities that facilitate terrorism, such as illicit financing and other crimes. The United States will continue to build capacity of foreign governments and non-government actors to credibly counter terrorist activities and narratives online through CVE programs.

Accomplishments:

- Launched State Department-led, whole-of-government cyber policy dialogues on the full range of issues with the European Union, Germany, India, Japan, and the Republic of Korea, among others, which complement the Department's ongoing digital economy policy dialogues with those countries, a whole-of-government ICT and Internet Working Group with Brazil, and new digital economy policy dialogues with Colombia and Taiwan, as well as a dialogue partnership with ASEAN. The Department of State, working with the interagency, regularly engages Australia, Canada, New Zealand, and the United Kingdom on cyber issues, and conducts regular bilateral discussions on cyber issues with numerous other countries around the world. The Department also initiated two regional cyber consultations in Europe that focus on cooperation in the Baltic countries and coordination in the Nordic-Baltic countries respectively; integrated cyber policy into existing mechanisms, such as the North American Leaders Summit and the Gulf Cooperation Council; and enhanced cyber-related dialogue with member states under the framework of the Organization of American States.

- Collaborated with the United Kingdom to launch the Global Conference on Cyberspace series in 2011, with the aim of expanding support for the vision articulated in the *International Strategy* among a like-minded community of governments, civil society groups, and private sector entities; and partnered with the governments of Hungary, the Netherlands, and the Republic of Korea to ensure additional successful conferences in 2012, 2013, and 2015.

- Integrated cyber policy issues into numerous ongoing political-military, strategic security, and human rights dialogues, including in Presidential-level bilateral discussions with Brazil, India, Japan, and the Republic of Korea.

- Utilized diplomatic channels, in conjunction with technical, law enforcement, and military engagements, when responding to serious cyber threats and incidents, such as the Sony Pictures incident in 2014 and the financial sector denial-of-service attacks in 2012-2013.

- Secured bilateral cyber commitments from China, following several years of high-level bilateral engagement, to: (1) develop constructive law enforcement cooperation on cyber-enabled crimes; (2) engage in high-level dialogue on cybercrime and network protection; (3) not conduct or knowingly support cyber-enabled theft of intellectual property, including trade secrets or other confidential business information, with the intent of providing competitive advantages to companies or commercial sectors; and (4) make common effort with the United States to further identify and promote appropriate norms of state behavior in cyberspace through an annual Senior Experts Group meeting led by the Department of State.

- Worked through the Global Counterterrorism Forum, which was established in September 2011, to counter the use of the Internet for terrorist purposes by developing and implementing international best practices regarding countering terrorist financing, promoting rule of law, responding to foreign terrorist fighters, countering violent extremism, and promoting violent extremist rehabilitation and reintegration.

- Sponsored and led the first-ever workshop on countering terrorist use of proxy actors in cyberspace in the ASEAN Regional Forum in 2012; sponsored workshops focused on countering online radicalization and recruitment to violence in India and Malaysia in 2015; and funded multilateral efforts to counter the use of the Internet for terrorist purposes in UN counterterrorism bodies, such as the UN Counter-Terrorism Committee, the Counter-Terrorism Implementation Task Force, and the UN Office on Drugs and Crime.

Mainstreaming Cyber Issues within the Department of State

The Department of State has devoted significant effort and resources to mainstreaming cyberspace issues into our foreign diplomatic engagements, as well as building the necessary internal capacity to formulate, coordinate, and implement cyber policy and execute our cyber diplomacy.

Accomplishments:

- Developed robust, tailored, regional bureau cyber strategies in 2012, and then fully revised them in 2014, to provide bureaus and U.S. Missions with a clear cyberspace policy game plan across each of the substantive pillars of the *International Strategy*, including capacity building.
- Integrated cyber issues into all core Department of State strategic planning documents, including the State and USAID Joint Strategic Plan (2014), the Quadrennial Diplomacy and Development Review (2010 and 2015), and the most recent Integrated Country Strategies; and launched a new "key issue" to track cyber-focused foreign assistance programming.
- Trained more than 150 officers, from more than 120 embassies and posts, on cyberspace policy via State Department-led interagency regional workshops in 2014 and 2015, and will train an additional 100 officers from embassies and posts in April 2016. Also trained more than 200 officers, from more than 70 embassies and posts, on Internet and telecommunications policy through an annual course at the Foreign Service Institute since 2011 and through regional trainings in 2014 and 2015.

Sec. 402(b)(2) – A plan of action to guide the diplomacy of the Secretary of State, with regard to foreign countries, including conducting bilateral and multilateral activities to develop the norms of responsible international behavior in cyberspace, and status review of existing discussions in multilateral fora to obtain agreements on international norms in cyberspace.

The United States has developed and is promoting a strategic framework of international cyber stability, designed to achieve and maintain a peaceful cyberspace environment where all states are able to fully realize its benefits, where there are advantages to cooperating against common threats and avoiding conflict, and where there is little incentive for states to engage in disruptive behavior or attack one another. There are three key elements to this framework: (1) global affirmation of the applicability of international law to state behavior in cyberspace; (2) the development of international consensus on additional norms and principles of responsible state behavior in cyberspace that apply during peacetime; and (3) the development and implementation of practical CBMs, which can help ensure stability in cyberspace by reducing the risk of misperception and escalation. We have forged a growing international consensus on this framework, and will continue to promote a broad consensus on international cyber stability wherever possible. Expanding and building on this consensus is a core diplomatic priority for the United States. To that end, the Department of State and the Administration have raised and will continue raising these issues at a high level in key bilateral and multilateral engagements with countries around the globe.

The United States developed this framework of cyber stability when the international community first began discussing the risks and threats posed to cyberspace by coercive state behavior. The President's *International Strategy* fully articulated and affirmed this approach. To achieve an international consensus around this framework, we have sought to develop a broad and diverse group of like-minded, responsible states – through discussion in expert-level forums followed by leaders-level commitments to key conclusions and recommendations – that recognize the benefits of affirming these principles. Since 2009, the **United Nations Group of Governmental Experts on Developments in the Field of Information and Telecommunications in the Context of International Security (UN GGE)** has served as a productive and groundbreaking expert-level venue to build support for this framework. The consensus recommendations of the three UN GGE reports (2010, 2013, and 2015) have set the standard for the international community on international cyberspace norms and CBMs. The UN GGE process will continue to play a central role in our efforts to fully promulgate this framework when it reconvenes in August 2016.

The United States made significant progress in promoting our strategic framework of international cyber stability in 2015. Leaders of the **Group of Twenty (G20)** issued a strong statement in 2015 reaffirming this U.S.-championed vision of international cyber stability and its pillars. The G20 leaders affirmed that international law applies to state behavior in cyberspace, and highlighted the work of the UN GGE and its 2015 report. In addition, building on a commitment made by China's President Xi in September 2015, G20 leaders also affirmed a U.S.-championed norm that no country should conduct or support the cyber-enabled theft of intellectual property, including trade secrets or other confidential business information, with the intent of providing competitive advantages to its companies or commercial sectors.

The first and most fundamental pillar of our framework for international cyber stability is the applicability of existing international law to state behavior in cyberspace. As noted above, the 2013 UN GGE report was a landmark achievement that affirmed the applicability of existing international law, including the UN Charter, to state conduct in cyberspace. The 2013 report underscored that states must act in cyberspace under the established international obligations and commitments that have guided their actions for decades – in peacetime and during conflict – and states must meet their international obligations regarding internationally wrongful acts attributable to them. All states are parties to the UN Charter, which seeks to prevent war of all kinds. They also must comply with their obligations under the law of armed conflict, including their obligations under the Geneva Convention, a body of law which is aimed at minimizing civilian suffering when armed conflict occurs. This law and other bodies of international law are a cornerstone of international relations, and are particularly important for cyberspace, where state-on-state activities are becoming more prevalent. The 2014-2015 UN GGE also made progress on issues related to international law by affirming the applicability of the inherent right to self-defense as recognized in Article 51 of the UN Charter, and noting the law of armed conflict's fundamental principles of humanity, necessity, proportionality, and distinction. We have achieved a broad consensus on the applicability of international law to state behavior in cyberspace. As we continue to promote this affirmation at the leaders-level and with a broad group of like-minded states, we also will continue to seek a more in-depth common articulation of how these principles apply to state conduct in cyberspace.

The United States is also building consensus on a set of additional, voluntary norms of responsible state behavior in cyberspace that define key areas of risk which would be of national and/or economic security concern to all states and which should be off-limits during times of peace. If observed, these stability measures – which are measures of self-restraint – can contribute substantially to conflict prevention and stability. The United States was the first state to propose a set of specific peacetime cyber norms, including the protection of critical infrastructure, the protection of CSIRTs, and cooperation between states in responding to appropriate requests in mitigating malicious cyber activity emanating from their territory, and, in May 2015, Secretary of State Kerry highlighted these norms in his speech in Seoul, South Korea, on an open and secure Internet. The 2015 UN GGE report's most significant achievement was its recommendations for voluntary norms of state behavior designed for peacetime, which included concepts championed by the United States. Another important norm in the UN GGE report calls on states to seek to prevent the proliferation of cyber tools that can be used for malicious purposes.

While these norms are voluntary in nature, they can serve to define an international standard of behavior to be observed by responsible like-minded states with the goal of preventing bad actors from engaging in malicious cyber activity. Over time, these norms can potentially provide a common platform for responsible states to preserve stability in response to state and non-state 'bad actors.' As a growing number of states commit to refrain from certain activities, states may be willing to join together to act against 'bad actors' to ensure there are consequences to bad behavior. Our future work on voluntary norms will consist of political-level affirmation of defined norms in a range of regional and international venues; further expert-level identification and articulation of additional stability measures that can also contribute to stability in peacetime, including via the next UN GGE process; and more expansive awareness-raising and engagement with a large and diverse group of actors: states with emerging and established cyber capabilities; other potential like-minded states; the CSIRT community; academia; critical infrastructure owners and operators; and other industry partners. In February, ASEAN leaders joined us in affirming their support for norms of state behavior in cyberspace at the US-ASEAN Special Leaders' Summit.

Together with our work on law and voluntary norms, cyber CBMs have the potential to contribute substantially to international cyber stability. CBMs have been used for decades to build confidence, reduce risk, and increase transparency in other areas of international concern. In order to develop the international framework for a technology which has no external observables and cannot be seen, cannot be counted, and where state capabilities cannot be easily assessed, we need to develop confidence that normal operating behavior by states is relatively predictable. Otherwise, any activity in cyberspace could lead to unintended consequences, miscalculation, or misattribution, thus increasing the risk of unintended conflict. Examples of cyber CBMs include: transparency measures, such as sharing national strategies or doctrine; cooperative measures, such as an initiative to combat a particular cyber incident or threat actor; and stability measures, such as committing to refrain from a certain activity of concern. Cyber CBMs are being developed, and are in the first stages of implementation, in two regional venues – the Organization for Security and Cooperation in Europe and the ASEAN Regional Forum – and we are encouraging other regional security venues to consider similar efforts.

In recent years, we have had great success in building international consensus as states coalesce around this framework. The relatively swift affirmation by states that international law applies to state behavior in cyberspace, their support for certain voluntary norms of state behavior, and their commitment to implement cyber CBMs in relevant venues, is notable and likely driven by an increased understanding among leaders and senior policymakers of the challenges and opportunities cyberspace presents to national security and foreign policy. Even if countries differ on a host of policy issues in cyberspace, all responsible states, whether developed or developing, can see a benefit to themselves and to increased use of cyberspace if this framework of international cyber stability gains wide-spread consensus. As cybersecurity becomes increasingly important to all states, the Department of State has sponsored a new international workshop series on cyber issues to bring a broader range of countries into the dialogue on cyber norms and international security in cyberspace and to help the lay the groundwork for the next UN GGE.

These Presidential priorities were underscored in the *Cybersecurity National Action Plan* released by the White House on February 9, 2016, which specifically stated the Administration's intent "to institutionalize and implement these norms through further bilateral and multilateral commitments and confidence building measures."

Sec. 402(b)(3) – A review of the alternative concepts with regard to international norms in cyberspace offered by foreign countries that are prominent actors, including China, Russia, Brazil, and India.

China and Russia pursue cyber policy imperatives that are often at odds with the United States and the broader international community. Their vision is for a system regulated by governments, contrasted with the U.S. vision of openness and collaborative, multistakeholder governance. Across all our engagements, the Department of State works to counter these alternative concepts, while working to promote the positive vision contained in the *International Strategy*.

China

China's approach to cyberspace in the international context is propelled by its desire to maintain internal stability, maintain sovereignty over its domestic cyberspace, and combat what it argues is an emerging cyber arms race and 'militarization' of cyberspace. This has led to a set of external policies that reinforces traditional Chinese foreign policy priorities of non-interference in internal affairs, sovereignty, and peaceful settlement of disputes. While the United States and its partners seek to focus our cyber policy efforts on combatting threats to networks, cyber infrastructure, and other physical threats from cyber tools, China also emphasizes the threats posed by online content. China views its expansive online censorship regime – including technologies such as the Great Firewall – as a necessary defense against destabilizing domestic and foreign influences, and it has promoted this conception internationally. These policies stand in sharp contrast to the U.S. view that all stakeholders should be able to contribute to the making of public policy regarding the Internet.

China has affirmed that international law applies in cyberspace, but has not been willing to affirm more specifically the applicability of the law of armed conflict or other laws of war, because it believes it would only serve to legitimize state use of cyber tools as weapons of war. Instead, China prefers to pursue further multilateral discussion of definitions, principles, and norms along with the creation of additional international regulations and a "Code of Conduct" at the United Nations that would seek to affirm total national sovereignty over content and cyber infrastructure within a country's borders. China further seeks to centralize adjudication of cyber-related issues in a UN context, as does Russia (discussed below).

China has been willing to consider cyber confidence building measures, but its lack of participation in CBMs in other contexts, in addition to its distrust of United States objectives, has prevented significant progress on practical bilateral cooperative measures to address strategic concerns. Following the U.S. indictment in May 2014 of five members of the Chinese military for cyber espionage for commercial advantage, China suspended the U.S.-China Cyber Working Group. However, as part of the recent cyber commitments between President Obama and President Xi, the United States and China pledged to establish a Senior Experts Group on international security issues in cyberspace, which will provide a forum to further engage China on its views and seek common ground regarding norms of state behavior in cyberspace and other topics, and which we currently are working to schedule. Additionally, as part of the cyber commitments, Attorney General Loretta Lynch and Homeland Security Secretary Jeh Johnson, together with Chinese State Councilor Guo Shengkun, co-chaired the first U.S.-China High-Level Joint Dialogue on Cybercrime and Related Issues to foster mutual understanding and enhance cooperation on law enforcement and network protection issues.

Russia

Russia's approach to cyberspace in the international context has also focused on the maintenance of internal stability, as well as sovereignty over its "information space". While Russia co-authored the Code of Conduct, with China and other Shanghai Cooperation Organization members, Russia's ultimate goal is an international convention, which would, *inter alia*, create new binding rules designed to limit the development, deployment, and use of "information weapons," promote speech and content controls, seek to replace the Budapest Convention's framework for combating cybercrime, and likely give the United Nations authority for determining attribution and responding to malicious cyber activity.

Russia has nonetheless found common ground with the United States approach of promoting the applicability of international law to state conduct in cyberspace, as well as voluntary, non-binding norms of state behavior in peacetime. Russia, which has previous experience in developing mechanisms for confidence building and maintaining strategic stability in other contexts, has also committed to the first-ever set of bilateral cyber confidence building measures with the United States, as well as the first set of cyber CBMs within a multilateral institution, at the Organization for Security and Cooperation in Europe, both in 2013 and 2016. Due to Russia's ongoing violation of Ukraine's sovereignty and territorial integrity, the United States has suspended our bilateral cyber dialogue with Russia. Nevertheless, we continue to interact with Russia on multilateral efforts to build greater stability and reduce the risk of conflict among states in cyberspace, including at the United Nations, the Organization for Security and Cooperation in Europe, and the ASEAN Regional Forum.

Russia and China are the most assertive states advancing alternative visions for international stability in cyberspace and seeking to sway undecided states in regional and multilateral venues. The United States counters proposals that conflict with our laws or cyberspace policy through a range of diplomatic tools, which include not only engagement in multilateral venues, but also direct bilateral engagement and awareness-raising with a variety of state and non-state actors. Even with these differences, the United States has been able to find common ground with Russia and China, as illustrated by the recent consensus reports of the UN GGE and the 2015 commitment at the G20 summit.

The United States works to advance our framework of international cyber stability alongside a broad group of like-minded countries, and in close collaboration with Brazil and India.

Brazil

The Brazilian approach to policy related to international security in cyberspace is shaped by a number of factors, including its emerging cyber military capabilities and policies, its membership in the BRICS and other affiliations, and its general preference for an expanded role for the United Nations. Brazil is a democratic nation with a strong belief in human rights and fundamental freedoms, including freedom of expression and the importance of international law, which factors into its willingness to affirm the applicability of international law to state behavior in cyberspace. Brazil has shown an increased interest in these issues, and served as an effective chair of the 2014-2015 UN GGE. The United States has a vibrant channel for engaging Brazil on international security issues, through the U.S.-Brazil Internet and ICT Working Group.

India

The United States has robust and growing engagements with India on cyber issues, including cyber norms, both bilaterally and in multilateral fora. India, which participated in the 2012-2013 UN GGE, and supported the 2015 G20 summit commitment, has voiced its support for the applicability of existing international law to state behavior in cyberspace. As the world's largest democracy, India also voices staunch support for freedom of expression online. Like many governments, the Indian government is concerned by the threats posed by use of the Internet for terrorist purposes, cybercrime, and the potential for objectionable Internet content to incite violence. The United States has a vibrant channel for engaging India on international security and other cyber policy issues, through the U.S.-India Cyber Dialogue.

Sec. 402(b)(4) – A detailed description of threats to United States national security in cyberspace from foreign countries, state-sponsored actors, and private actors to Federal and private sector infrastructure of the United States, intellectual property in the United States, and the privacy of citizens of the United States.

Cyber threats to United States national and economic security are increasing in frequency, scale, sophistication, and severity. Overall, the unclassified information and communication technology networks supporting U.S. government, military, commercial, and social activities remain vulnerable to espionage and disruption. The likelihood, however, of a catastrophic attack against the United States from any particular actor is remote at this time. The intelligence community (IC) instead foresees an ongoing series of low-to-moderate level cyber operations from a variety of sources, which will impose cumulative costs on U.S. economic competitiveness and national security, pose risks to federal and private sector infrastructure in the United States, infringe upon the rights of U.S. intellectual property holders, and violate the privacy of U.S. citizens.

Numerous actors remain undeterred from conducting economic cyber espionage or perpetrating cyber attacks. The IC continues to witness an increase in the scale and scope of reporting on malicious cyber activity that can be measured by the amount of corporate data stolen or deleted, personally identifiable information compromised, or remediation costs incurred by U.S. victims. The motivation to conduct cyber attacks and cyber espionage will probably remain strong because of the gains for the perpetrators.

These threats are discussed in greater detail in the classified Annex accompanying this Strategy.

Sec. 402(b)(5) – A review of policy tools available to the President to deter foreign countries, state-sponsored actors, and private actors, including those outlined in Executive Order 13694, released on April 1, 2015.

The United States works to counter threats in cyberspace through a whole-of-government approach that brings to bear its full range of instruments of national power and corresponding policy tools – diplomatic, informational, military, economic, intelligence, and law enforcement – as appropriate and consistent with applicable law. The United States believes deterrence in cyberspace is best accomplished through a combination of "deterrence by denial" – reducing the incentive of potential adversaries to use cyber capabilities against the United States by persuading them that the United States can deny their objectives – and "deterrence through cost imposition" – threatening or carrying out actions to inflict penalties and costs against adversaries that conduct malicious cyber activity against the United States. It is important to note there is no one-size-fits-all approach to deterring or responding to cyber threats. Rather, the individual characteristics of a particular threat determine the tools that would most appropriately be used.

The President has at his disposal a number of tools to carry out deterrence by denial. These include a range of policies, regulations, and voluntary standards aimed at increasing the security and resiliency of U.S. government and private sector computer systems. They also include incident response capabilities and certain law enforcement authorities, such as those used by the Department of Justice to take down criminal botnets. They include cyber threat information sharing mechanisms, as well as public-private partnerships. International cooperation is also a key element of the United States' strategy to respond to and prevent cyber incidents. The Department of Homeland Security's National Cybersecurity and Communications Integration Center (NCCIC) and law enforcement agencies frequently engage foreign counterparts to share information and coordinate operational assistance in responding to and mitigating malicious activities taking place from abroad. The Department of State can use its diplomatic channels, where appropriate, to bring a whole-of-government response to particular cyber incidents, and promote cooperation among policy makers in addressing these incidents.

With respect to cost imposition, the President is also able to draw on a range of response options from across the U.S. government.

- **Diplomatic tools** provide a way to communicate to adversaries when their actions are unacceptable and to build support and greater cooperation among, or seek assistance from, allies and like-minded countries to address shared threats. Diplomatic démarches to both friendly and potentially hostile states have become a regular component of the United States' response to major international cyber incidents. In the longer term, U.S. efforts to promote principles of responsible state behavior in cyberspace, including peacetime norms, are intended to build increasing consensus among like-minded states that can form a basis for cooperative responses to irresponsible state actions. We also emphasize and prioritize efforts to build cybersecurity and improve capacity to combat cybercrime in developing nations, which are increasingly targeted by transnational organized crime.

- **Law enforcement tools** can be used to investigate crimes and prosecute malicious cyber actors both within the United States and abroad. International cooperation is critical to cybercrime investigations, which is why the United States has promoted international harmonization of substantive and procedural cybercrime laws through the Budapest Convention, created an informal channel for data preservation and information sharing through the G7 24/7 network, and promoted donor partnerships to assist developing nations. U.S. law enforcement agencies regularly work with a wide range of partner countries to apprehend and extradite cyber criminals for prosecution in the United States or a third-party country. The Department of State's Transnational Organized Crime Rewards Program directly supports law enforcement efforts to bring significant cyber criminals to justice by offering rewards for information leading to the arrest or conviction of suspected members and leaders of Internet-based criminal organizations.

- **Economic tools**, such as economic sanctions, offer another option for responding to, and imposing costs on, malicious actors in cyberspace. In January 2015, in response to North Korea's destructive and coercive attack on Sony Pictures Entertainment, the Administration announced new sanctions on certain North Korean actors; the North Korea Sanctions and Policy Enhancement Act of 2016 offers additional country-specific tools. Moreover, in April 2015, the President issued Executive Order 13694, *Blocking the Property of Certain Persons Engaging in Significant Malicious Cyber-Enabled Activities*, which authorizes the imposition of sanctions on individuals and entities whose engagement in certain malicious cyber-enabled activities poses a significant threat to the national security, foreign policy, economic health, or financial stability of the Unites States.

- **Military capabilities** also provide an important set of options for deterring and responding to malicious cyber activity. As with all of the other tools described above, the United States has made clear for some time that just because an attack takes place in cyberspace does not mean a lawful and appropriate response must be conducted through cyber means. The President's *International Strategy* discussed this policy, and the 2015 *Department of Defense Cyber Strategy* states: "The United States will continue to respond to cyberattacks against U.S. interests at a time, in a manner, and in a place of our choosing, using appropriate instruments of U.S. power and in accordance with applicable law." The Department of Defense continues to build its cyber capabilities and strengthen its cyber defense and deterrence posture. As part of this effort, the Department of Defense is building its Cyber Mission Force of 133 teams to be fully operational by the end of 2018. The Cyber Mission Force, which already is employing capabilities, will defend Department of Defense networks, defend the Nation against cyberattacks of significant consequence, and generate integrated cyberspace effects in support of operational plans and contingency operations.

- **Intelligence capabilities** are also an important tool at the President's disposal in detecting, responding to, and deterring malicious activities in cyberspace, particularly given the unique challenges associated with attributing and understanding the motivation behind malicious activities in cyberspace.

Even with this broad range of tools, deterring cyber threats remains a challenge. Given the unique characteristics of cyberspace, the United States continues to work to develop additional and appropriate consequences it can impose on malicious actors.

Additional information on U.S. cyber deterrence policy can be found in a report on cyber deterrence that the Administration submitted to Congress in 2015, pursuant to section 941 of the Fiscal Year 2014 National Defense Authorization Act.

Sec. 402(b)(6) – A review of resources required by the Secretary, including the Office of the Coordinator for Cyber Issues, to conduct activities to build responsible norms of international cyber behavior.

The Department of State effectively utilizes the resources provided through the annual federal budget process to conduct its diplomatic activities in support of this Strategy and the President's *International Strategy for Cyberspace*.

Specifically, the Office of the Coordinator for Cyber Issues effectively utilizes its resources, including leveraging Diplomatic and Consular Program (D&CP) and foreign assistance funds, to carry out its coordination role to strengthen and expand diplomatic activities, and to develop and implement capacity building programs that improve cybersecurity due diligence globally, combat cybercrime, and build international security in cyberspace.

Our ability to fight transnational cybercrime and respond to foreign cyber threats is greatly enhanced by the capabilities and strength of our international partners in this area. Thus, the Department of State is working with allies and multilateral partners to build the capacity of foreign governments, particularly in developing countries, to secure their own networks, as well as investigate and prosecute cybercriminals within their borders. Additionally, the Office of the Coordinator for Cyber Issues is spearheading the effort to promote international consensus that existing international law applies to state actions in cyberspace and build support for certain peacetime norms through assisting states in developing technical capabilities and relevant laws and policies, to ensure they are able to properly meet their commitments on norms of international cyber behavior.

Taking into consideration the rapidly expanding environment of global cyber threats and the reality that many developing nations are still in the early stages of their cyber maturity, the Department of State anticipates a continued increase and expansion of our cyber-focused diplomatic efforts for the foreseeable future, which will require additional resources for both increased diplomatic engagement and enhanced foreign assistance support for capacity building. The Department remains appreciative of continued Congressional support of its authorities and budgetary resources in this priority area.

ISBN 9781542705325

90000 >